Slow Down and Walk:
A Conversation

Nadine George-Graves
& Okwui Okpokwasili

In August 2020, during a global pandemic and ongoing uprisings against systemic racism and police brutality in the wake of George Floyd's murder on May 25, Nadine George-Graves—scholar, director, dramaturg, choreographer and Chair of the Department of Dance at Ohio State University—met on zoom with Okwui Okpokwasili—writer, dancer, performance maker, and choreographer—as part of the "50WomenAtYale150" series.

The two women—friends who are deeply aligned in thinking about ways to reconfigure and reimagine the performative space—met to discuss Okpokwasili's performance and installation, Sitting on a Man's Head, *created with her husband and partner Peter Born as part of the Danspace Project 2020 Platform:* Utterances from the Chorus, *a program that was cut short by the shutdown of New York City in March 2020. Building on ideas of shared practice and reoriented relationships between audience and performers, Okpokwasili's and George-Graves's conversation considers new and radical modes of being together and caring for each other, both in artistic practice and in how that practice can extend into the rest of our lives. Their dialogue invites us to entertain the notion that, even amidst the most ungenerous circumstances of our changing world, daring to be generous—perhaps even virtuosically—can open the possibility to renewed curiosity and surprise.*

This talk was co-sponsored by Yale Women, the Yale Alumni Association, and the Yale Black Alumni Association, with technical assistance from Wendy Maldonado D'Amico.

Nadine George-Graves: Good afternoon, everyone. Today I have the pleasure of introducing our featured speaker and my beloved friend Okwui, a Brooklyn-based multi-disciplinary performer. On a personal note, I've known Okwui since college. And I've always been in awe of her brilliance and deep commitment to her work as an artist. I was thinking of how to introduce you, Okwui, and I remember working with you in college, on *Jesus Christ Superstar*. I choreographed it, and you played, I think, Judas Iscariot.

Okwui Okpokwasili: *[Laughing]* Yeah, I did.

NGG: I remember beautifully choreographing every five, six, seven. eight. There might have been a jazz hand or two.

OO: Yeah, there may have been.

NGG: And I got to you, Okwui, and I was just like, "You know what? Okwui, you just go." And I think that says a lot right there. So I'm honored to be in conversation with you. And I want to thank you so much for being here. Let's start. Yale asked me to ask you first to talk about your Yale days, your time as a student, how that might have influenced your artistic journey. Is there anything you want to say about yourself and pivotal moments that got you here?

OO: First of all, I want to say, thank you. It is an honor to be here at Yale, fifty years honoring women at Yale college, and one hundred and fifty years honoring women at the university. And speaking to you, my dear Nadine George-Graves, who is an incredible mover, maker, artist, rigorous intellect herself around performance. So the one thing I'll say about Yale is that I think what was really, really important in my development and growth were the resources that they gave to undergraduates to make their own work. To do these experiments like *Jesus Christ Superstar*. Was it in Morse, I think? You know what I mean? That was funded by the Yale Dramat, right? Which is this incredible resource for all of us at the different colleges where we get access to funds to make our own productions. And I used those resources, often, to do my work, and to do collaborative work with others. I think that was just super. It was singular and very significant in thinking about the capacity to make work and thinking and realizing that I had the capacity to make work and also thinking collaboratively in a big way. I mean, I feel like not only did I do that—I remember also working with people on their own projects, particularly there was Ronobir Lahiri, who was Yale '94. He did a version of the *Ramayana* and it happened outside. I think it was the Saybrook and J. E. Courtyard? I think he utilized both. One was kind of grass. One was stone. And actually during the course of this piece, we moved through the courtyards. I hope that answers the question.

NGG: I'm in this—and we can talk about our little worlds, you know. I've been teaching undergrads for a while and I think that there is a sense of maybe, maybe a little bit of entitlement—let's, let's be real, you know, Yale has the money—but also just freedom, to do what we do without really knowing the rules sometimes. Well, it's also having the resources. I run up against, often, undergrads who didn't get cast in the main stage and then they're like, "Oh, well, guess I'm not going to perform." And I'm like—especially when I was in San Diego—"It's warm! Go outside, do something," you know? So maybe there's something, you know, important about that permission and those resources that are available, but also just the blissful ignorance of not necessarily knowing that you weren't supposed to do things without a grownup's permission.

OO: Exactly. And I think, you know, sometimes we took inspiration from text, we were looking at the Living Theater, we were reading about the experiments of the Wooster Group. We were reading Suzan-Lori Parks. We were looking at all of these people who were in some way trying to reformulate, rethink how work is made from not just the text and the form and shape of the actual performative product, but also in terms of the strategies of making work. The strategies of thinking about, okay, how do we reflect on what we are doing as art makers, a kind of imagination about how we want to live in the world, right?

Like how does the work that we make perhaps send a signal or start to plant a seed for other ways of living that aren't predatory, that aren't purely transactional, that are grounded in an idea of building art and culture, but also thinking about care. And, you know, just thinking like imagining having a space to imagine things you may not have seen, but definitely dream about, that are also beyond your own immediate desire for gratification or, I don't know, it's not just about developing a product to be sold, right? But there's a whole ethos around what it means to come together and build something together that speaks to something larger about a community. Like when you look at the people around you, not just as agents of your own vision, but as collaborators in visions that you might not have imagined, but they can inspire you to think even bigger than you had thought. Not just like, "Ooh, I'm going to make this *brilliant* show." You know? No, it's like, what if, what if we looked at each other as all possessing the capacity to…

NGG: Fill in the blank? Right?

OO: To fill in the blank, but actually, sometimes, I feel like I can be overly careful with language, but sometimes I feel like I spew. And so I'm toggling between, is that really the word? But I feel like everybody has a contribution to make, right. And I'm thinking about, you know, you might say, "Oh, this is a lighting designer. They're an amazing lighting designer." But maybe they come in and have something really essential to say about sound, right?

NGG: Thank you, thank you.

OO: Or something to say, you know, or someone comes into the piece and you thought they were a choreographer, but maybe they have an incredible dramaturgical impulse that you should follow. Right? Because just how do you allow, how do you make space for the people that come in as collaborators with you to kind of keep bursting the bonds of how you think you should be working and constantly making you reconfigure relationship. Like being open to that. And I just feel like all of the collaborative relationships that I started to build at Yale—some of them that I continue to this day, and especially my husband, he also went to Yale and we were collabrators—so just constantly allow yourself to be surprised. Allow your curiosity to be piqued, allow yourself to be pushed beyond what you imagined was possible.

NGG: You make it sound so easy, right?

OO: No, it's very... stressful.

NGG: Yeah. And also it feels like it should be easy. And there's a way in which, there is this impetus to perhaps have a mastery of form. So I'm virtuosic in this technique, in this form and by these parameters and by this definition. And what happens when the commitment to that form doesn't allow for other things to happen? Right? And how do we measure virtuosity in other ways? So how are you virtuosic as a collaborator? How are you virtuosic in allowing the work to be what it is without imposing rules or definitions on top of it from the beginning? Or how are you virtuosic in recognizing the stakes, how are you virtuosic in your generosity of yourself and your honesty. Right? And I think, and I will say sometimes, you know, the stakes are high, and things are dangerous. Things get out of control. I believe we burned that—we burned it down.

OO: Mm-hmm. We burned it down. Yeah. I feel like at the Afro-Am house, I feel so bad. I remember we would go in there and we were working on a piece and I remember I was like smoking cigarettes in there. And I can't remember the name of the incredible dean who was there. She was like, "Can you not do that?" But you know, we're, we're experimenting, and we just, we were feeling free and feeling ourselves and it's true. Sometimes you're like, okay, what are the limits of that freedom? You know what I mean?

But you know, I also think that there's a responsibility that we have to each other to just kind of, I don't know, I'm just thinking of Suzuki, right? Like the Zen beginner mind. How to always kind of, how to have a beginner's mind about all of it. And so maybe that means... Do we have to discard ideas about virtuosity? Do you know what I mean? Like how do we divorce virtuosity or ideas of perfection from... Or, I don't know, is virtuosity...you know, I started thinking about Noh performance, right? This like ancient and thousands and thousands, thousands years old practice, right? Where people are kind of doing the same, ostensibly the same, thing. They have a very, very strict and very specific container that they have to inhabit. Right? But, you know, the way they inhabit that, those particular possibilities, maybe the movement of how the head moves is maybe very uniquely and individually their own. And so there is a potential for a kind of virtuosity and also a spirit to transmit through this very, very strict container. So now I'm like, well, I guess we don't have to discard virtuosity *so* much, but I guess I'm not interested in virtuosity. I'm interested in practice and I am interested—

NGG: Yes. You just also happened to be virtuosic. I'm going to say it out loud.

OO: That's why I be loving you Nadine. That's why I be loving you.

NGG: Yeah, you walk into the room virtuosically, but what I'm also hearing is this recognition of other possibilities that might be…rhythm? That might be an energy, might be something else that we value, as opposed to, you know, getting your leg up to here. And I think that that's part of what people are recognizing in your work, even when we can't quite articulate in a review, what she's doing, what the genre is, what that means, but like, *oh my God*, that was amazing.

OO: But it's not just what *I* do. It's not just what I do. There's a whole container around that. I like working with collaborators.

NGG: Right, but it's what you bring out. It wouldn't happen without you.

OO: That's true, because there's a dynamic conversation that I'm having with my collaborators and all of the elements of the piece.

NGG: So I've been told that I should go to the clip, because we're just chit-chatting.

OO: Oh, sorry. You know, Nadine and I were supposed to go have a coffee. Back in pre-COVID days.

NGG: Yes. That's right. So this is really just our coffee talk.

NGG: The last time we saw each other face to face was in January at the Gibney . Yes. We saw a performance. You came to a performance of *Afro/Solo/Man*[1] that I dramaturged and I moderated a discussion and I'm thinking about that moment here because I think that was another moment where I realized how important the audience is to creating—I'm going to say out loud—a ritual *and* a performance. And that's really connecting me to you and your work and what can happen in your performance. And so the clip that we chose is from a performance that really speaks to that, right? It brings you in—all of your work brings people in.

OO: It's a practice.

NGG: It's a practice. And I'm going to say sometimes your work, I must say, sometimes it is *excruciating*.

OO: Good! *[laughs]*

NGG: But it is always powerful. It's always powerful. And so were going to talk about this piece and your work [over coffee] and then the world fell apart...several times. So we're picking up, and maybe we can watch this and think about ritual, theatrical dance practices, spaces for recognition and restoration. The clip is from the performance I *didn't* get to see [live] in March called *Sitting on a Man's Head*[2] that happened at the Danspace Project. And I think it is getting at these conversations about rhythm and what's possible, and who we are as performers and audience members, and blurring those lines.

OO: Yeah, it's a practice really. I mean, it was an attempt actually to do a *non*-performance. An attempt to sort of start to build modes of being with strangers in sacred ways, in creative ways, to make space for the utterances that people need, you know, to emit.

[technical difficulties showing clip from Sitting on a Man's Head*]*

OO: No problem. This is an attempt to build a chorus as we sing it. I love it.

Wendy Maldonado D'Amico: Why is it not playing?

OO: This is *zoom*, that's why.

WMD: It's always zoom's fault, right?

OO: So people are speaking in the chat. I'm going to look in the chat, y'all. Somebody has made a suggestion for a solution for this in the chat. I guess this is kind of what I like about this. Nothing is really too serious right now. We're all here. We all know. We've all had our technical issues with zoom.

NGG: And there's this radical forgiveness, I think, for awhile. So my students, in March, radically forgave me, as I tried to figure out how zoom worked, I became one of those old professors, "Oh, I don't know how this works." I became one of the old professors. I don't think they're going to forgive me as much in the fall.

WMD: I don't know why this isn't working and I'm so embarrassed.

OO: No, please don't be. We can also skip it because you know what? I can just talk about it. And people can please go check out the clip, maybe we'll put a link to it, you know, because it's really, it's not really anything—to be perfectly honest with you. It's not something spectacular; it's not a spectacle. We designed something, it actually was my first time co-curating an exhibition that happens with Danspace Project. It's a place of performance, but there have been ten platforms designed since 2010 that are basically these ongoing exhibitions over the course of five weeks around a particular line of inquiry.

They've done things like *Lost and Found*, which was considering the works of artists who passed away from AIDS. How have we lost them? How are we finding them? Asking artists to sort of re-engage with some of the works of those folks. There was another platform, *Dancing Platform Praying Grounds,* considering how sites of worship have shaped religious, African diasporic and postmodern dance practices over the centuries. The curatorial investigation uncovered the invisible and vanished bodies who built St. Mark's church in the city—namely the slaves, the enslaved people who built the church. *This* platform (or the platform I co-curated) was designed around the chorus: what are the possibilities, as a community, for us to come together, to sing together, to speak together, to cry together? Is it possible—one of the questions was—is it possible for us to utter together, to shape and weave a sonic space together?

So, there are a number of ways in which the platform or this exhibition tried to make space for shared artistic practice, possibilities of engaging the public and building different types of relationship with audience. All of these ways where we are trying to ask: what are ways that we can creatively take care of each other, listen to each other with generosity? With almost an *unbearable* generosity.

WMD: Let me, let me try and share this once more, one more time, ladies. I'm just stubborn.

OO: That's the Yale lady way.

NGG: Do not accept defeat. We're going to get an "A" in zoom.

OO: So we can see it, but we can't hear it for some reason. It's all right, love. Okay. I feel you, Wendy. No worries at all.

WMD: We'll send out the link to the video.

NGG: I was going to say—I say this to my students about lots of things, and I'll say this to all of us—let's put our finger on our pulse. Right? So put your finger on your pulse right now. Wendy, put your finger on your pulse. It's probably racing. Let it go. What does that mean? What does it mean about our expectations? About what zoom's supposed to be and what a clip during a webinar's supposed to look like and what does it mean that now, we're going to listen to them talk about something that I didn't get to witness *right now*. I'm going to have to be patient and wait and give myself the practice of actually going and clicking on it myself later on, and then think back to what they talked about. Right? What does that mean? And how do we allow that to be what it is right now, too?

I was going to mention this article called, "It Matters for Whom You Dance."[3] And it's about a lot of things, but I think it says a lot in the title. Because there's something about who's in the space with you. And, you know, those of us who are performers know that sometimes it was a great night and the audience was totally with us, but there are other kinds of performances that just don't exist without a certain kind of commitment by the audience. That's what I was going to talk about after we saw the clip—that commitment. And how are there real profound possibilities for that? And then also slowness.

OO: Yes, yes. But also the sense of forgiving yourself. Letting go and forgiveness. And then opening yourself up to what's actually happening now. What's here. To not get stuck on what could have been or what was supposed to be happening, right? But to see the gift that's in front of you right now.

NGG: And also take some improv classes! Take some improv classes because you have the script—I've got the script, but the clip doesn't work. You have to have a conversation and be able to trust. I trust you. I said to Okwui last night, 10 o'clock. What are we going to talk about? I said, "I'm just going to say nice shirt and you're going to just talk and it'll be brilliant." And I knew it would be.

OO: And I decided also not to wear a shirt.

NGG: I knew you were going to not wear a shirt because of that. Nice necklace.

OO: Cowrie shells baby.

NGG: Oh, beautiful. I've got mine. Should I go get mine?

OO: Yeah. Do you want to get yours?

NGG: Yeah. You talk. You talk about slowness and time and patience.

OO: And I mean, I will say yes. Go get your cowrie shells. *[laughs]* So I will tell you all too, that the process of this particular practice was that there would be no audience. People would come into the space and have the opportunity to either sit with a book that asked individuals a question and ask them to address this question. Which is: What do you carry and how in turn does that carry you?

[NGG comes back with cowrie shell necklace]

You see, the cowrie shell is the vagina of the deep, right? It's a signal. It just keeps reminding us from where we come, the first channel, the first opening.

Anyway, you would move into the space. And you would either address a question in the book privately, which was, what do you carry and how in turn does that carry you? Or you would move to another part of the space and just sit and listen to the sound outside.

If you chose to address this question—What do you carry and how in turn does that carry you?—one of the artist activators, one of the people in the practice, would come out and have a conversation with you about what you had written. And then with whatever content or language generated from this conversation, you would walk to another threshold that would lead you into another interior space where you would do a slow walk and start to take a kind of account of breath, your breath and the breath of those around you, and be with them in the space and then see how that conversation and language reverberated within you, but also in relationship to the sound that was happening in the space already. And so the idea was that once you decided to have this conversation and walk through the threshold into the space and lend your piece to this sonic weave, there was no audience, right? There was just you and your fellow collaborators and practitioners. And so what happens in the clip, in the beginning it starts out, you might recognize that it's just the artist activators, who were my collaborators in building the piece. And then as it grows, you also begin to see the public and the guests who entered into the practice, you would see it would get bigger. So you couldn't necessarily see who the artists were and who the guests were. We were all engaged in a collaborative practice with each other and it was private and it was sacred and it was actually, it was—especially in this time, the fact that it was happening before the breath of others could be lethal to you. I miss it acutely. I miss that practice acutely.

NGG: And it might've seemed small as a concept: "What, I'm going to walk through a room next to people?" But think about that now. The idea of breathing together, walking through a room...

OO: And sounding together. And how does that sound? And yes, sometimes there might've been lyrics, but sometimes there were screams and shouts and laughs. And when we went back to look at the video, it was astounding because there was so much spoken about breath. Give me breath. God! And then I was looking at this with my partner—who's also my husband—and it was just astounding to be looking at this video and putting this clip together in the wake of George Floyd's murder.

And I do believe that there are things that we all carry with each other. There are certain common threads that we carry, and that the fact that this rose up in this time... It took my breath away.

NGG: I'm writing this mini monograph. It might be published—right now, it's all just in my diary—titled *How I Got Through the Trump Years by Watching Black Dance*.

OO: Yes. I love that.

NGG: And I hope there's only one volume. There's only going to be one volume...

OO: Please, Lord. Please.

NGG: ...chronicling the last four years of my practice of turning to Blackness and our art to get me through each month. And I will say, you figure prominently in many, many months, including this, and slowness, and *For Colored Girls*.[4] Because I'm thinking of all of our Brown and Black precious "colored" children whom we've failed profoundly and miserably, deeply, and what we have for them, what we are offering them. And I think about one of my favorite Okwui moments (that we don't have time to talk about) is that talk that you gave at BAM when somebody said—talking about institutions, remember this?

OO: Yes.

NGG: "Okay, so how do you think about white people when you work and, you know, institutions, and where's the whiteness in your work, and what do you think about white people?" And you were like, "I *don't*. Next question."

So, I'm thinking about Blackness, and performance, and the ongoing disaster of the American political landscape, and this horrific moment, and it is too much to take on. And—Wendy's telling me I've got like, two minutes before I have to let other people talk to you—which I might just not do, maybe that's a practice, like, I take over the webinar: "There will be no Q&A!"

OO: Resistance, refusal.

NGG: But how do we sustain ourselves and how do you—that's not fair to ask you—but how are you sustaining yourself as an artist *right now*? As you know, I'm in mourning for... what you just said. I'm in mourning for that... maybe, I went to Catholic school, that time before the fall, when we could do something simple, like come together and breathe together. Because this machine is grinding us to dust, girl, as Audre Lorde said, so we're going to talk anyway. And in two minutes we might let somebody else talk, but... What does it mean?

OO: Nadine, I adore you.

NGG: Blackness!

OO: I want you to keep talking. I want you to talk about the work that you're looking at.

NGG: Blackness. Blackness. All that and Black people. No pressure.

OO: You know there was a Rahsaan Roland Kirk album... I forget, but I feel like it was like *[sings]* "B-L-A-C-K! B-L-A-C-K! "BLACKNESS." Does anyone know that? It was so great.

NGG: I think we're making people uncomfortable. Don't make them uncomfortable!

OO: Just listen to that song. I would loop that shit. "B-L-A-C-K!"

NGG: Okwui, don't make people uncomfortable! You're going to hurt their feelings!

OO: Nobody's uncomfortable. Everyone here went to Yale. Most of you are relatively privileged, and maybe struggling a bit. Hey, I understand that, I'm living in my rent-stabilized apartment. But we're all right. We're going to be okay.

NGG: Okay, you talk. I'm going to mute.

OO: No, don't you do that.

Why don't you just open it up to folks, because Nadine, I have to say, I think that's incredible. And the work that you dramaturged, *Afro/Solo/Man*—I'm thinking about Orlando Hunter and Ricarrdo Valentine, and the space that you gave them to engage in ritual, that was as much about pain, but also their love for each other as HIV-positive men, to think about them falling in love, right? And how they had to make the space for that love. And I felt like you helped us move through rituals where they had to cleanse themselves of all of the things that wanted to keep them from loving each other. It was so, so beautiful. I mean, it was hilarious. I mean, I think there were many, many levels of the piece, but we talked about how even if I couldn't signify, what are some of the… Maybe I couldn't decode exactly the signs and symbols and the rituals that I was watching, right? Like in the dust or covering yourself in the white, even though I feel like that has to do with this trying to move into the ancestor realm again. I still felt some kind of ineffable, energetic movement, right? And it was holding me and taking me and opening me, and I thought, I'm so glad that they worked with you to give that space, to do that, to be there. Can you talk about that?

NGG: No, because you know what, Okwui, I'm going to cry. So, I'm going to say, I should put myself on mute, because this is what I do. I perform. Right? I am an introvert, I'm a shy kid, and I perform, but you know, you're right. We were getting to places in the stakes, right? Because this is not a luxury for us. For me. It's not a luxury. And the things that we're talking about—what we can afford, what's possible through our performance—when we get there, when we do the things that you're talking about, when we can create a ritual, when we can make the space in a room, especially for people, for whom space and voice is a battle in other rooms, or who don't exist in other spaces—

OO: See, this is the thing. I feel like people do not realize. People are always like, "Why is everybody bitching? Why are people so angry? Blah, blah, blah." I'm like, do you understand that people are out here marching, and they're crying out, and they're trying to open up space and detoxify? Yes, for their own liberation, but *you too* will be liberated. You, too. You, too. That energetic flow, that river will carry you somewhere, right? People just walk around thinking about, "Oh, that motherfucker over there wants my shit." Nobody wants your shit! Nobody wants to take shit from you, because you don't have the thing that they need.

NGG: And also, we probably built that shit anyway. I built that shit!

OO: We built that shit anyway, but it's this idea of so many people who want to hold on to the paltry little bits that they've been given as if it was gold, and they don't realize. I don't want your shit. I'm making space for you to start to think about a new relationship, not just to me, but even to yourself and the world that will give you a—that you won't even—the fucking gift that you'll get from that is *way* beyond anything that you can imagine. Right? I don't want to get all Star Trek and shit, but damn…let's get on with this! Let's not just be stuck in these old fights. And if people are sick, if your neighbor is sick, *you will get sick*. Chances are, you will get sick. Or if your neighbor cannot afford their house and leaves it to rot, that rot will reach you. It's so… I don't know. Anyway.

NGG: I'm going to do my job, Okwui. From Wendy: "Nadine, did you *see* the first question?"

OO: [laughs] "Nadine, did you *see* the first question?"

NGG: No, she did not emphasize the "see." The "see" was very polite. *I* put the emphasis on the "see."

OO: And that's the thing about women. Like, we haven't even talked yet about the significance of women, right? Look at Jacinda Ardern in New Zealand, Angela Merkel in Germany. The collaborative work that women are doing to bring healing and safety to their communities is a freaking model that all these other fuckers need to like, sit down and bow down to. Come to the table with their notebooks open, mouths shut, and take some notes. Boom. Boom!

NGG: We could tie this to institutions and freedom and who's saying and speaking your mind... and you know what I'm going to do though, I'm going to tie it all together, because that's what I do as a teacher. So, all of that and gender, and someone asked you about being a mother. Pregnancy, birth... I will bring it back to "If you're a mom how did movement affect your experience of pregnancy and birth?"

OO: It was amazing. Yeah, that was amazing. You know, I was fortunate enough to not have a lot of issues after pregnancy. And my daughter is quite healthy. She was born early—premature. I like to also point out that, you know, my parents were first generation, and my mother's first two children—my brothers were born late and then on time, and I just feel like it didn't even take generations for her to start to have deeply premature babies. I was born in my seventh month. And I have a sister below me who was born in her sixth month. Then my other sister was born in her seventh month. And I started to think about the impact and stress of structural racism on my mother that, you know, she started to fall into those categories where Black women are disproportionately endangered by our medical system.

My daughter was a little bit premature. We were in intensive care. She was in the NICU. Came out healthy. I have to say that it was amazing, because I felt my body as a resource in a way that I had never felt it before. All she needed was for me to eat, take care of myself. And all she needed was my good, strong, sturdy breast milk, and I could latch her on to me and move through the world, and she would be fine. And so that was really, really exciting and empowering for me. And I think that sometimes I move around the world in a way that could be described as ignorant or courageous, but there are a lot of institutions where I was making work, and I would bring my daughter. I was just bringing her. I wasn't asking anyone if I could bring her, I wasn't being like, "Oh, what's this going to do to my career if I bring her"—it wasn't a question. If I was in the room, if I had to be in the room, she was coming with me. Because there was no way in hell I was leaving my four-month-old daughter while I'd be somewhere for six or seven hours. Or while I'd be traveling to work on a piece—there was no way in hell. And so I wonder about… I know that there are a lot of women who really have to consider what it means to have a child in relationship to a particular career trajectory. But sometimes—I have to say—that we must stop asking and just do it. But I know it's complicated. I'm not in banking. You know what I mean? I'm not a corporate lawyer, so I know that there are certain strictures that are different. But hey, we've seen Tammy Duckworth breastfeed her child in the halls of Congress, so let's give it a shot.

NGG: There is a question about blood and memory... blood memory, and how that animates your work. She asked particularly because she's "currently completing a dual timeline novel, told through a Black girl, a woman who has an encounter with an experience of her four mothers, and that blood memory animates her body, even when she cannot speak, speak it, or remember it in a conscious way." So, blood memory and animating your work.

OO: It animates it. Oh, that's the only thing that I'm interested in. You know, but of course, I also believe that those are some among the ineffable things that we might feel, but may not be able to articulate. So I try in my practice of making movement to create containers around duration and slowness to see if I could also activate some of those deep cellular memories, these blood memories. To instruct me. I don't necessarily say that this is exactly what it is. But I am trying to access and open up some channel that I know is in relationship to all of the ways that the women and the people who have come before me are implanted in me, are in me in some way. But I think that, yes, I don't know that I can address that question or answer it in any other way that's satisfying.

NGG: So, you know, there's a question about, I think, traveling the world... "As creatives who have traveled the world, your experience with non-U.S. audiences' reaction and/or relationship with Blackness," and I'm going to tie that to a question about "advice that you have for people who have lost their performance communities, or communities, in general due to the pandemic." Collaboration, building community, so…what does community mean? Who are you connecting with before, internationally, and now, during the pandemic? I'm going to throw in all of those other plagues, too. The plague of white supremacy, the plague of Trump.

OO: Patriarchy.

NGG: Patriarchy.

OO: I can't say his name, the grifter-in-chief.

NGG: Don't say it.

OO: Oh my gosh, talk about teaching your child lessons around forgiveness. My husband today, we were listening to something and he said something and our daughter was like, "Well, we have to be forgiving." He was like, "You can't forgive someone that doesn't acknowledge that what they're doing is toxic and wrong! Those people just need to be punished." And I was like, "Meh. Good point." But then again, I'm like, "What? If he stood up and apologized, then what? You still going to jail, motherfucker." I hope. That's off topic.

I'll see if I can address this thing. You know, the pieces that I've done around the world in different countries, there's no monolith. I think that sometimes—there's a particular solo piece I did called *Bronx Gothic*. And I did that in Paris, and then in Strasburg and Croatia. Markedly different experiences across those three countries. Australia. And it's really interesting. I think that a lot of the people of color, Black folk, Indigenous folk, when you are out of the country, particularly in France and dealing with a lot of like Francophone people who are connected to the former French colonies in Africa, and also in North Africa and Algeria. And sometimes they really feel like, they were like, "*Thank you.*" Because these countries still have not made spaces in their institutions for our voices, which is maybe shifting. Right? It's always interesting to me when I go to places like Germany and France, and all of their spaces that do make room, and they understand the importance of a kind of cultural lineage, legacy, and so they do support that through public funds. And also they have their social safety nets, which are much more generous than ours.

So, there are so many ways that I feel like they should be models for us, but in other ways, I think that when they think about racism, systemic racism, they really think that the U.S. is a unique space, where these are problems, right? Where I think—and I believe what's emerging now—is that no, the U.S. is unique in that we have built so many rigorous institutions around fighting for civil rights and fighting for opportunity, that we have been models around the world. And so it seems like we have been inspiring, that the United States has been inspiring all of these folks in other countries to actually rise up and lift up their voice and speak to the way that they've been marginalized or made invisible, or the way their concerns have been discarded. There is a way in which the colonial, there was a way in which, especially back in what I feel like were the early aughts, when I was first starting to really travel, in places like Germany—I feel like I was somewhere, at the House of World Cultures, even, I think was built in the West and JFK—maybe he didn't speak there, but he may have gone there, they have a room dedicated to him. I'm sorry, now I'm not remembering. I remember speaking to a woman who seemed really lovely, a German woman, and she was like, "Oh, it's so terrible. The racism in your country." And then in her second breath, she talked about the dirty Turkish people sitting down, and I said, "Whoa, cognitive dissonance." I was like, "Why did you just ascribe dirtiness to Turkish people and their children?" She's like, "Well, no, they are, they come in here and they do this stuff." And I'm like, "First of all, they've been in your country for a long time. And why do you sit here with the confidence to say this to me? Do you understand that this is racism? This is xenophobia. You are making this huge generalization about an entire culture that can't possibly be proven." You know? And also, "What is it about your generalization, *right now*, that is creating conditions that actually confirm the thing that you believe." And she was like, "Oh, you don't understand. You don't know." And we got into this thing.

NGG: Why does she think that you would be receptive to that? Why does she think that, "Surely, you'll understand"?

OO: It was such *blindness*, such blindness. Just even last year, I was at some fancy dinner some place with some people somewhere, I don't remember exactly. And they were like, "Oh yeah, England is..."—they were talking about how different England is or London is, you know—"racism doesn't exist there," or something. And it was a white woman talking to me. A white American woman who lives in Brooklyn. And I said to her, "What? I know people from the UK." And she was like, "Well, *I've* never heard it." I was like, "Well, who would be talking to *you* about it?" It was crazy, right? Or you go to the Netherlands, and it's like *blinders*. This is the thing about going to Europe, you know? I'm always like, "Check yourself. You know the triangular trade, right? And you? In the Netherlands? You better step back. Do you know who King Leopold is? I'm so glad you can fund my project. But I'm slightly complicit now."

NGG: "Just sign the check. Thanks for the grant."

OO: But I'm still slightly complicit that you built wealth on the bodies of the folks in the Congo. So, I feel like what's really interesting about this moment is that it is making all of these folks in Europe also have to kind of...or maybe not. I don't know. Maybe not. Maybe not.

NGG: That was right on. I'm going to ask this last question—two more: "Can you speak about your days of learning to trust yourself, your voice as an artist?" And then—oh, this is real: "I'm fighting a sense of despair as a performance artist right now. I'm wondering, what your strategies are for staying passionate and invested in your work when we don't know when we will see each other in person again?" Those are good questions to end.

OO: And also that ties into the thing I didn't address around community. Where's your community, building community.

First of all, like "When do you learn to trust yourself as an artist? When did you learn? How do you do this?" I don't know. I almost can't even ask myself that question. I don't always, you know what I mean? I make stuff, I make stuff, I go, and I go, and I look at it. I have collaborators or I'm alone. I'm looking at it, I'm looking at it, and I say, sometimes I'm like, "This is what I've got. I'm going to offer it with humility and gratitude." And then, you know, leave it up to…I don't know.

And as to "What is performance right now? Live performance community?" It's almost like you have to let go of any ideas—at least for me—around community. I try not to hold on to this idea of, "Well, you're my tribe. You're my tribe. *You're* my tribe." There are definitely people that you're in closer contact with. There are definitely people that you're checking in on. But there are also people I haven't spoken to in years that reached out, and I'm kind of like, "Hey! Where are you? How are you?" There are people that pop up in my mind, and I'm like, "I'm just going to send an email." "What you doing? Where are you living right now?" Can community sort of encompass that? Can we let go of all of the expectations we have?

Because I think community is not even just about people who are next to you, but it's just about people who pop up in your heart. People that you remember. People that maybe you're not next to all of the time, but they reside in you.

NGG: It feels like that's also the answer to that question about fighting despair during this time.

OO: Yes. But also, sometimes also giving into despair, you know? I mean, don't jump off of a roof. Because that does nothing, right? Except end everything and end all possibility of moving out of this darkness and using it as a lesson.

NGG: Acknowledge the trauma. This is traumatizing. The whole world is traumatized.

OO: *Yes.* Yes.

NGG: And we have to acknowledge that and sit in it. Right? We're always like, "Keep teaching, keep learning, keep researching..." Or *not*. Or just chill out and be patient, and wait for the scientists to get it right [and find a cure].

OO: That's right. Exactly. We're acknowledging the trauma of also how we built this country. What is this country? This time...like, maybe COVID is a gift—it's given us this... Okay, sit here with all of this death, sit here with all of the ways in which we don't take care of each other. Do we have an opportunity to start taking care of each other? It's like people who don't worry about being innocent, don't worry about...Just encounter all of the things that are dark, that hurt. Sit with them, move through them. Let them be your teachers, right? I don't know. I *don't know*.

NGG: I'm going to end there, because you know what...

OO: Sorry, we're way over time.

NGG: We're not over time. We're at time. I'm very good at this. We're at time.

OO: You are damn good at this.

NGG: That was a beautiful way to end, because you know what? There's a part of me—the teacher in me—that wants to give people a hopeful note and to end as a cheerleader. I was voted the most outstanding cheerleader in eighth grade, I just want everybody to know that. But like the outfit's at the dry cleaners—I keep saying. We're going to end there. I think we're ending up sitting in the trauma and letting it be what it is.

OO: You've got to ride it through.

NGG: That's radical. Radical forgiveness and radical acceptance, and still being an artist and being who we need to be.

Let us give praise to our teachers, and COVID is the teacher. Despair as a teacher.

NGG: How was that, Okwui? Was that good?

OO: Outstanding. And it's also a standing ovation.

References

1   Brother(hood) Dance! *Afro/Solo/Man*. January 11, 2020. The Theater at Gibney, New York City.

2   Okwui Okpokwasili and Peter Born. *Sitting on a Man's Head*. March 2020. Danspace Project, New York City.

3   Coorlawala, Uttara Asha. "It Matters For Whom You Dance: Audience Participation in *Rasa* Theory," in *Dance Matters*, ed. Pallabi Chakravorty and Nilanjana Gupta. (New Delhi and London: Routledge, 2010).

4   *For Colored Girls Who Have Considered Suicide / When the Rainbow is Enuf!* by Ntozake Shange, directed by Leah C. Gardiner. October–December 2019. The Public Theater, New York City. Okpokwasili played the Lady in Green.

Slow Down and Walk: A Conversation
Copyright © Nadine George-Graves & Okwui Okpokwasili, 2020

Adapted from "Slow Down and Walk with Okwui Okpokwasili,"
a video interview presented by 50WomenAtYale150, which can
be viewed at: vimeo.com/showcase/6912610/video/449376541.

2020 Pamphlet Series
ISBN 978-1-946433-53-4
First Edition, First Printing
Edition of 1,000

Ugly Duckling Presse
The Old American Can Factory
232 Third Street, #E-303
Brooklyn, NY 11215
uglyducklingpresse.org

Distributed in the USA by SPD/Small Press Distribution
Distributed in the UK by Inpress Books

Series design by chuck kuan and Sarah Lawson
Typeset by Wen Zhuang
Type is New Century Schoolbook
Cover paper and flyleaf from French Paper Co.
Printed offset and bound at McNaughton & Gunn
Flyleaf printed letterpress at Ugly Duckling Presse

This publication was made possible, in part, by support
from the New York State Council on the Arts, a state agency,
and by public funds from the New York City Department of
Cultural Affairs in partnership with the City Council. This
project is supported by the Robert Rauschenberg Foundation.

This pamphlet is part of UDP's 2020 Pamphlet Series: twenty commissioned essays on poetics, translation, performance, collective work, pedagogy, and small press publishing. The authors are listed below; their pamphlets are available for individual purchase and as a subscription (uglyducklingpresse.org/subscribe). Each offers a different approach to the pamphlet as a form of working in the present, an engagement at once sustained and ephemeral.

Mirene Arsanios
~~Omar Berrada~~*
Sergio Chejfec
Don Mee Choi
Kunci Study Forum & Collective
Iris Cushing
Simon Cutts
Nicole Cecilia Delgado
Adjua Gargi Nzinga Greaves
Dimitra Ioannou

Sibyl Kempson
Claudia La Rocco
Aditi Machado
Chantal Maillard
Tinashe Mushakavanhu
Sawako Nakayasu
Tammy Nguyen
Aleksandr Skidan
Steven Zultanski
Magdalena Zurawski

*Nadine George-Graves & Okwui Okpokwasili

To win a subscription, write to office@uglyducklingpresse.org with your solution to the following puzzle: Using only 6 straight lines, divide the circle on the back cover so that each number is in its own section, without any overlap between numbers.